MW01504254

**Copyright 2024**
**ISBN 979-8-9915**

Rev. Date; 08/17/2024

Edited: Janice Extrom

Artwork: Jeorge Mercardo

To order copies of this book, go to Amazon.com and search this title.

"Bob Brooks' passion for military history is on full display by providing this veteran history workbook making it a fantastic contribution to capturing our distinguished veteran's experiences and military history in an easy fill in the blanks approach. Bob expertly provides a series of thoughtful questions that the military historian or family member can use to interview the veteran illuminating and permanently capturing the veterans' experiences and honorable service to this nation. If you have a veteran in your family, this workbook is a must have."

COL (R) John Norris

# Tell me all you can about your service.

---

Stories bring history to life, and this workbook aims to do just that. If you are a Veteran or a family member of a Veteran, you are part of a unique group. As of November 2023, over 18 million Veterans live in the United States, making up just six percent of the population. That's 18 million stories that need to be shared.[1]

This workbook is designed to help Veterans share their stories and preserve their legacies. Families often want to know more about their loved one's military service, especially if they have sacrificed greatly for their country. This workbook helps Veterans tell their unique stories in their own voice.

For those not in the military, service can be intriguing, sometimes leading to awkward or intrusive questions. This workbook is not meant to make anyone uncomfortable. Veterans have the right to decide what to share. This book provides a private way to pass on their history, ensuring memories aren't lost.

Some Veterans might choose to complete this workbook for their family for the time after they've passed. Others may prefer not to discuss their service verbally but are willing to write about it. The amount shared is up to the Veteran. This is their history as they lived it.

Some family members will have questions after their Veteran has passed. This workbook can provide a valuable record and guide for researching their service. Knowing the right questions to ask is crucial.

It is hoped that Veterans and their families will use this workbook to share their stories. The information provided can aid further research by family members. Some may even use this book to write a more detailed biography of their time in service. This is encouraged, and there will be no issues with using this book for personal purposes only. What matters most are the memories and history being preserved.

**"History, once lost, can never be recovered to the same level of accuracy as the passing of time takes its toll. Don't let it be lost to antiquity."**

**(Robert J. Brooks)**

---

1 Schaeffer. "The changing face of America's veteran population." Pew Research Center. November 8, 2023. https://pewrsr.ch/3yH3sd8.

**What are your vital statistics? (Where and when you were born, what hospital, etc.)**

_____

_____

_____

_____

_____

_____

_____

_____

_____

_____

_____

_____

_____

_____

_____

_____

_____

# What are your parent's names? What can you tell us about their history?

_____

_____

_____

_____

_____

_____

_____

_____

_____

_____

_____

_____

_____

_____

_____

_____

**What made you interested in the military? Why did you join or were you drafted?**

_____

_____

_____

_____

_____

_____

_____

_____

_____

_____

_____

_____

_____

_____

_____

_____

**Describe your education. Include names of schools, locations, and dates you were there.**

_____

_____

_____

_____

_____

_____

_____

_____

_____

_____

_____

_____

_____

_____

_____

_____

**Were you in ROTC? What are some of your memories of that time?**

_____

_____

_____

_____

_____

_____

_____

_____

_____

_____

_____

_____

_____

_____

_____

_____

## What Branch did you decide to join and why?

_____

_____

_____

_____

_____

_____

_____

_____

_____

_____

_____

_____

_____

_____

_____

**What is your military ID/Serial Number in case its needed to connect with the National Archive (NARA)? Privacy is respected and you need not answer.**

_____

_____

_____

_____

_____

_____

_____

_____

_____

_____

_____

_____

_____

_____

## How did your contract read? What was your Reserve Service obligation?

_____

_____

_____

_____

_____

_____

_____

_____

_____

_____

_____

_____

_____

_____

_____

_____

# What did your friends think about you joining the service?

_____

_____

_____

_____

_____

_____

_____

_____

_____

_____

_____

_____

_____

_____

_____

## Did anyone in your family serve, and if so, what Branches?

_____

_____

_____

_____

_____

_____

_____

_____

_____

_____

_____

_____

_____

_____

**If you enlisted, what was in your contract to serve, and how long were you obligated in Reserve?**

_____

_____

_____

_____

_____

_____

_____

_____

_____

_____

_____

_____

_____

_____

_____

_____

## What did your parents think about you going into the service?

_____

_____

_____

_____

_____

_____

_____

_____

_____

_____

_____

_____

_____

_____

_____

_____

## Where did you do your Basic Training and what do you remember of that time?

_____

_____

_____

_____

_____

_____

_____

_____

_____

_____

_____

_____

_____

_____

_____

_____

_____

**Do you recall your graduating class from Basic, and is there a photo?**

_____

_____

_____

_____

_____

_____

_____

_____

_____

_____

_____

_____

_____

_____

**What major events were happening globally or on a national level when you entered into service?**

_____

_____

_____

_____

_____

_____

_____

_____

_____

_____

_____

_____

_____

_____

_____

_____

**Where did you do your Advance Individual Training (AIT) and what was that MOS?**

_____

_____

_____

_____

_____

_____

_____

_____

_____

_____

_____

_____

_____

_____

_____

_____

## Did you have a specific MOS that you wanted or did they assign you?

_____

_____

_____

_____

_____

_____

_____

_____

_____

_____

_____

_____

_____

_____

# Are there any stories from AIT that you remember?

_____

_____

_____

_____

_____

_____

_____

_____

_____

_____

_____

_____

_____

_____

**Did you make any friends that you are still in contact with from those early years in Basic or AIT? If so, what were their names, where did you meet them, and what is their address?**

_____

_____

_____

_____

_____

_____

_____

_____

_____

_____

_____

_____

_____

_____

_____

**Is there a story that you would think is the funniest thing to happen while in AIT?**

_____

_____

_____

_____

_____

_____

_____

_____

_____

_____

_____

_____

_____

_____

_____

**Joining up, describe any preconceived
notions that you may have had about
serving in the military.**

_____

_____

_____

_____

_____

_____

_____

_____

_____

_____

_____

_____

_____

_____

_____

_____

# What was the biggest surprise once you were in uniform?

_____

_____

_____

_____

_____

_____

_____

_____

_____

_____

_____

_____

_____

_____

_____

_____

# What was your biggest disappointment once you were in uniform?

_____

_____

_____

_____

_____

_____

_____

_____

_____

_____

_____

_____

_____

_____

_____

_____

**Do you still have a copy of your DD214 or are you still in commitment with the government?**

_____

_____

_____

_____

_____

_____

_____

_____

_____

_____

_____

_____

_____

_____

_____

# Did you have any regrets for joining up?

## Did your significant other think about you joining?

_____

_____

_____

_____

_____

_____

_____

_____

_____

_____

_____

_____

_____

_____

_____

**What unit were you assigned to after AIT? Did you have a choice in the matter?**

_____

_____

_____

_____

_____

_____

_____

_____

_____

_____

_____

_____

_____

_____

_____

_____

## Did you ever leave the country as part of the military?

_____

_____

_____

_____

_____

_____

_____

_____

_____

_____

_____

_____

_____

_____

_____

## Are you a Combat Veteran? What units, Division, Regiment, Battalion, Company?

_____

_____

_____

_____

_____

_____

_____

_____

_____

_____

_____

_____

_____

_____

_____

# Were you ever assigned to a TDY (Temporary Duty Station)? What and where was it?

_____

_____

_____

_____

_____

_____

_____

_____

_____

_____

_____

_____

_____

_____

_____

## What other training did you take after AIT?

_____

_____

_____

_____

_____

_____

_____

_____

_____

_____

_____

_____

_____

_____

_____

_____

_____

## List ranks and dates that you achieved them?

_____

_____

_____

_____

_____

_____

_____

_____

_____

_____

_____

_____

_____

_____

_____

_____

_____

# What is your funniest story while in uniform?

_____

_____

_____

_____

_____

_____

_____

_____

_____

_____

_____

_____

_____

_____

_____

_____

**What bases did you go to while in service, and what can you tell me about being those times?**

_____

_____

_____

_____

_____

_____

_____

_____

_____

_____

_____

_____

_____

_____

_____

_____

# What jobs did you pursue in the military and why?

_____

_____

_____

_____

_____

_____

_____

_____

_____

_____

_____

_____

_____

_____

_____

_____

**Did you have a second choice as an MOS when you
signed up, and what was it?**

_____

_____

_____

_____

_____

_____

_____

_____

_____

_____

_____

_____

_____

_____

_____

_____

_____

# What was the most important thing you learned from Basic?

_____

_____

_____

_____

_____

_____

_____

_____

_____

_____

_____

_____

_____

_____

_____

## What was instilled in you as a Veteran that still holds sway with you today?

_____

_____

_____

_____

_____

_____

_____

_____

_____

_____

_____

_____

_____

_____

_____

_____

**If the military requested you to reenlist would you go, and why?**

_____

_____

_____

_____

_____

_____

_____

_____

_____

_____

_____

_____

_____

_____

_____

_____

_____

# What was the most mentally challenging part of training?

_____

_____

_____

_____

_____

_____

_____

_____

_____

_____

_____

_____

_____

_____

_____

**Did you find the military to be more difficult mentally or physically?**

_____

_____

_____

_____

_____

_____

_____

_____

_____

_____

_____

_____

_____

_____

_____

_____

**If you could do it all over again, would you do it, and what might you change if anything?**

_____

_____

_____

_____

_____

_____

_____

_____

_____

_____

_____

_____

_____

_____

_____

_____

# What makes a good or bad soldier?

_____

_____

_____

_____

_____

_____

_____

_____

_____

_____

_____

_____

_____

_____

_____

_____

**What does "Mission First" mean to you?**

_____

_____

_____

_____

_____

_____

_____

_____

_____

_____

_____

_____

_____

_____

_____

_____

**What do the military core values mean to you?
Loyalty, Duty, Respect, Honor, Integrity, Personal
Courage.**

## What does "I will always maintain my military bearing" mean to you?

_____

_____

_____

_____

_____

_____

_____

_____

_____

_____

_____

_____

_____

_____

**What does the warrior ethos mean to you? "I will never quit, accept defeat, or leave a soldier behind."**

_____

_____

_____

_____

_____

_____

_____

_____

_____

_____

_____

_____

_____

_____

**What does military courtesy mean to you? (ie., How to give an officer your honest opinion when you disagree.") Have you ever given an officer your opinion?**

_____

_____

_____

_____

_____

_____

_____

_____

_____

_____

_____

_____

_____

_____

_____

**Permission to speak freely. (A story
goes here that we have not asked a
question about)**

_____

_____

_____

_____

_____

_____

_____

_____

_____

_____

_____

_____

_____

_____

_____

_____

_____

**Has serving in the military helped you with working with others? (Team building, adapt, improvise, and overcome)**

_____

_____

_____

_____

_____

_____

_____

_____

_____

_____

_____

_____

_____

_____

_____

_____

_____

_____

**Do you remember the three general orders?**

_____

_____

_____

_____

_____

_____

_____

_____

_____

_____

_____

_____

_____

_____

_____

_____

# Why can't you wear your cover indoors?

_____

_____

_____

_____

_____

_____

_____

_____

_____

_____

_____

_____

_____

_____

_____

_____

**What was it like going through the gas chamber?**

_____

_____

_____

_____

_____

_____

_____

_____

_____

_____

_____

_____

_____

_____

_____

_____

**What was your take on field training at the end of Basic? (Omaha Beach-grenade throwing, low crawling-live fire exercises)**

_____

_____

_____

_____

_____

_____

_____

_____

_____

_____

_____

_____

_____

_____

_____

_____

_____

## What is your opinion on war?

_____

_____

_____

_____

_____

_____

_____

_____

_____

_____

_____

_____

_____

_____

_____

_____

_____

**Did you ever think you were brainwashed?**

_____

_____

_____

_____

_____

_____

_____

_____

_____

_____

_____

_____

_____

_____

_____

_____

**Did you have any hand-to-hand combat experience? Describe it for us if you can?**

# What is Close Quarter Combat with a rifle and no ammo?

___

___

___

___

___

___

___

___

___

___

___

___

___

___

___

___

# How many weeks did you spend on learning to handle a rifle?

_____

_____

_____

_____

_____

_____

_____

_____

_____

_____

_____

_____

_____

_____

_____

_____

**Tell us about being disciplined. How many push-ups could you, or did you do?**

_____

_____

_____

_____

_____

_____

_____

_____

_____

_____

_____

_____

_____

_____

_____

_____

_____

**Tell us about "Getting Smoked"
during the "Shark Attack" if it
applies.**

_____

_____

_____

_____

_____

_____

_____

_____

_____

_____

_____

_____

_____

_____

_____

_____

**What was the best base that you
traveled to and why? In your opinion,
what made it the best?**

_____

_____

_____

_____

_____

_____

_____

_____

_____

_____

_____

_____

_____

_____

_____

_____

_____

_____

# What was the worst base that you traveled to and why?

_____

_____

_____

_____

_____

_____

_____

_____

_____

_____

_____

_____

_____

_____

_____

**If you could go back in time and re-enter the military, what would you tell your younger self?**

_____

_____

_____

_____

_____

_____

_____

_____

_____

_____

_____

_____

_____

_____

_____

_____

_____

_____

**Are there any stories about your leave time or downtime that you would share?**

_____

_____

_____

_____

_____

_____

_____

_____

_____

_____

_____

_____

_____

_____

_____

_____

_____

# Was shining boots therapeutic?

## How many different Regiments/Battalions/Companies were you assigned to in your career?

_____

_____

_____

_____

_____

_____

_____

_____

_____

_____

_____

_____

_____

_____

_____

_____

**Do you know the dates/locations when assigned to those units referenced in the previous question?**

_____

_____

_____

_____

_____

_____

_____

_____

_____

_____

_____

_____

_____

_____

_____

_____

_____

**Are there any questions that haven't been asked that you would like to speak about?**

_____

_____

_____

_____

_____

_____

_____

_____

_____

_____

_____

_____

_____

_____

_____

# What did the service represent or mean to you?

_____

_____

_____

_____

_____

_____

_____

_____

_____

_____

_____

_____

_____

_____

_____

_____

**If you were a short timer, why did you decided to get out or were you injured out and how?**

_____

_____

_____

_____

_____

_____

_____

_____

_____

_____

_____

_____

_____

_____

_____

_____

**As you moved up in rank, did you have an idea of how far you wanted to go?**

# Are there any officers you worked with who reached a high level of notoriety?

_____

_____

_____

_____

_____

_____

_____

_____

_____

_____

_____

_____

_____

_____

_____

_____

_____

**Tell us about the awards you received and why?**

_____

_____

_____

_____

_____

_____

_____

_____

_____

_____

_____

_____

_____

_____

_____

_____

_____

**Is there an NCO or Officer in your command who really stands out to you and why?**

_____

_____

_____

_____

_____

_____

_____

_____

_____

_____

_____

_____

_____

_____

_____

**Is there an NCO or Officer who was influential to you during your service? Name and describe as many as you like.**

_____

_____

_____

_____

_____

_____

_____

_____

_____

_____

_____

_____

_____

_____

_____

_____

## Who were some of your Commanding Officers and what did you think of them?

_____

_____

_____

_____

_____

_____

_____

_____

_____

_____

_____

_____

_____

_____

_____

## What Campaigns were you involved in? (as well as dates or locations)

_____

_____

_____

_____

_____

_____

_____

_____

_____

_____

_____

_____

_____

_____

_____

_____

# Who had the most influence on you to join the military?

_____

_____

_____

_____

_____

_____

_____

_____

_____

_____

_____

_____

_____

_____

_____

_____

# What was the hardest thing you ever had to do in the military?

_____

_____

_____

_____

_____

_____

_____

_____

_____

_____

_____

_____

_____

_____

_____

_____

_____

# Did you bring home any spoils of war or souvenirs from foreign countries?

_____

_____

_____

_____

_____

_____

_____

_____

_____

_____

_____

_____

_____

_____

_____

**Describe life in a combat zone if you served in one and what were your first impressions?**

_____

_____

_____

_____

_____

_____

_____

_____

_____

_____

_____

_____

_____

_____

_____

_____

# Will you describe life in the field?

_____

_____

_____

_____

_____

_____

_____

_____

_____

_____

_____

_____

_____

_____

_____

_____

_____

**Describe your life or issues you may have had within your Regiment/Battalion/Company.**

_____

_____

_____

_____

_____

_____

_____

_____

_____

_____

_____

_____

_____

_____

_____

_____

_____

## What were your personal goals once you left the military?

_____

_____

_____

_____

_____

_____

_____

_____

_____

_____

_____

_____

_____

_____

_____

_____

_____

## Are there any questions that were not asked that you would like to speak to?

_____

_____

_____

_____

_____

_____

_____

_____

_____

_____

_____

_____

_____

_____

_____

_____

_____

**Is there anything that you wish your family to know about you or that you want them to remember or understand?**

_____

_____

_____

_____

_____

_____

_____

_____

_____

_____

_____

_____

_____

_____

_____

# Additional Space

**Be sure to note the page number of the question you are continuing on with here.**

_____

_____

_____

_____

_____

_____

_____

_____

_____

_____

_____

_____

_____

_____

_____

_____

# Research Links

National Archives-Veterans' Service Records
https://www.archives.gov/

Office of Naval Research, CTR
Department of the Navy
875 N. Randolph Street
Arlington, Va 22203

US Army Installation Management Command
https://home.army.mil/imcom/index.php/garrisons

US Army Human Resources Command HRC
https://www.hrc.army.mil/content/Army%20Service
%20Center

General US Army HR Request.
usarmy.knox.hrc.mbx.tagd-ask-hrc@army.mil.

The Air Force & Space Force IP Management Team
Air Force Public Affairs Agency
Comm: 210-652-6058 (DSN: 665-6058)

United States Marine Corps.
HQMC, Counsel for the Commandant
Office: 703-784-6859
Cell: 571-732-7968

The Korean War Project
https://www.koreanwar.org/

The Korean War Educator
https://www.thekwe.org/

Thanks go to the following for their help and suggestions in the creation of this transcript.

**Sharon Extrom** (Daughter of Korean War Veteran)
**Robert McQuillan US Army** (Vietnam War combat Veteran)
**Jeorge Mercardo US Army** (Artwork and Cover)
**James Green US Army Retired** (Cold War era)
**Robert Wilson US Army Retired** (Combat Veteran War on Terror)
**Johnny Babbs US Army** (Vietnam War Combat Veteran)
**Chris Peeks US Army** (War on Terror Combat Veteran)
**Sam Arredondo US Army Ret.** (WWII, Korea, Vietnam Veteran)

Special thanks **to Janice Sheridan** for her continued tutelage whose guidance made this project come in.

To **Ray Vallowe US Army** (Korean War) friend and author whose valuable teachings continue to serve me still.
*What History Failed to Record*

To **Dwight R. Rider Senior Master Sgt. US Air Force Ret.** whose friendship and guidance through the years has shown this author how to research in better ways to better serve.
*Hog Wild-1945*

To **CSM Ray Hooker Cottrell US Army Ret.** for creating the starting point from which all of this came to be.

To **CSM Elliot Sortillo US Army Ret.** (Korean War POW) whose friendship will never be Forgotten.

To **Adrienne Moss** from whose support I could not do any of the things I do.

Made in the USA
Las Vegas, NV
24 October 2024

10423538R00059